CHERISHED MEMORIES

An inspiring book depicting God's love and His wonderful plan of salvation for all mankind.

BY ESLYN GLASGOW

Copyright © 2024 by Eslyn Glasgow

All rights reserved. Use of any part of this publication reproduced, transmitted in any form or by any electronic or mechanical means including information storage and retrieval systems requires written permission from the copyright holder, except by a reviewer who may quote brief passages in review.

Cherished Memories / Eslyn Glasgow

All scripture references in this book are taken from the King James Version.

Uncited photographs are from the author's private collection

Cover photo: Emjay Andrews

Printed and bound in Canada by Hignell Book Printing

ISBN: 978-1-77835-225-6

Contents

Dedication v

In Appreciation of Cherished Memories vii

One: *My Life as a Child* 1

Two: *Teenage Years* 9

Three: *Transition:*
From Sheltered Life to Cruel World 21

Four: *Young Adult:*
Falling In Love 29

Five: *Married Life:*
Encounter with Jesus 35

Six: *Family Life:*
Along Came the Babies 43

Family Photos 52

Seven & Eight: *Accounts of God's*
Divine Intervention 63

Nine: *Synopsis:*
Reaching out to the Reader 83

Epilogue 89

Acknowledgments 91

DEDICATION

*I wish to dedicate this book to my household:
To my husband Joe, my children Justin (Lisa),
Jacinth & Shelley (Dave).*

*Also, to my six grandchildren: Jackson, Brooklyn,
Talia, Jacob, Emjay, and Kaliyah.*

*This book chronicles my life as a child, my life as
a grown woman, and my walk with the Lord.*

*My hope is that everyone who reads this book will be
blessed, inspired spiritually, and that faith will arise
in their hearts.*

Read on and enjoy!

In Appreciation of Cherished Memories

The style is natural and easy to read. It clearly comes from the heart and does not come across as something professionally done, this makes it more real and believable. The humanity it displays will be an important attraction to the readers who may see themselves in these experiences. I am quite sure it will provide encouragement to others. Your testimonies will draw many to the Lord.
— *Hamid O'Brien*

I read your book last night. It is very good! It's uplifting. I enjoyed getting to know you better, while being introduced to a country and culture different from the one in which I grew up. I also related to living in Winnipeg, attending Calvary Temple and also living a life in Christ. You have simply but eloquently shown the path of salvation through Jesus Christ.
— *Debbie Stewart*

You have indeed shined the light in this way so that anyone who reads this book will surely come to a decision. You have been very sound in the word of God and have an appropriateness with the invitation to lead to the Lord those who will read your testimony. It is excellent how you explained and summarized your convictions at the end. There is a clear invitation to all who read your memoir to accept the Lord, particularly with the inclusion of the Salvation Scriptures.
— *Phillip Charles*

One

The walk through the large living room seemed endless. Traversing that room always struck fear into me: There was no one to be seen, yet there was a man's voice speaking each time I passed by. I hurried from the room as fast as I could and silently wished that my mom would refrain from ever visiting that home again; strange things were taking place there. That was my harsh introduction to the radio at the age of three when our family lived in the village of Toco, Trinidad. Why didn't someone explain to me that the voice I heard, actually came through wires that were attached to the box on the mantelpiece.

The next clear recollection of my childhood places me in Black Rock, Tobago in the year 1952. The scenario unfolds: It is the end of the school day. I am six years old. My dad who is the principal of the Black Rock Moravian School gets ready to transport us home to Plymouth on his bicycle. I remember myself and my two older sisters wearing beautiful felt hats with velvet ribbons tied around our necks; mine was a deep red almost burgundy in colour. I do not know how he did it, but I remember my dad skilfully navigating his way through the narrow streets, with my sister Valerie riding on the handlebar, my sister Vestine on the carrier behind him, and me on the crossbar directly in front of him, all the way to Plymouth. At home we were greeted by my mom and younger sisters Allison and Cilda who were happy to see us arrive. As far as I know at that time the rides were fun for everyone, as we chatted and sometimes sang all the three miles to our home. It is only recently as I began writing this memoir, that my sister Valerie shared with me the paralyzing fear that gripped her as she rode on the handlebars. She stated that she always feared she would fall off, whenever my dad briskly pedalled downhill.

If I were asked to describe my childhood in two words, it would be "extremely happy." I was the third child in a family of five girls. There was always laughter and song in our home. My dad loved to sing. He possessed a harmonious and melodious voice and we just loved to sing along with him. Unfortunately, my mom was not blessed with a voice for singing. She was unable to carry a tune correctly, however, she too will join in whenever we had our impromptu concerts, and we would quietly laugh when she sang her favourite tune, in her high-pitched voice, way off key. We all had our special songs for the "concert nights." My second sister Vestine was always an Elvis Presley fan as she sang "Your Loving Teddy Bear" complete with action and all. While my sisters sang one or two stanzas of their favourite songs; when it was my turn, I insisted on singing all five stanzas of my song much to their provocation. I was good at mass memorization and felt that cutting short my song would not do justice to myself or to the song. It was a song that my dad had taught me, entitled "A Spanish Cavalier." It had an interesting storyline, and I felt I just had to sing every last line.

Our bike rides came to an end in 1954 when my dad purchased a brand-new green automobile, a Ford Consul. We called it "the consul." In those days automobiles were scarce. There must have been no more than three cars in the entire village. We soon realized that our car proved to be a Godsend to the villagers. In reading my dad's eulogy in July 2002, my sister Cilda described it as the village ambulance. I clearly recall as a young child, at all hours of the night, we would hear people's voices calling out to our dad, "Good night Mr. Grant" or "Good night teach," as he was affectionately called because of his profession.

We kids soon began to understand that these late-night calls meant that people were in some type of distress and needed my dad to transport them to the hospital, which was about five miles away in the capital city of Scarborough. Sometimes it would be husbands whose wives were in childbirth labour or some other emergency. One morning I heard my dad relating to my mom his experience the previous night. This particular woman he was transporting to the hospital was having an asthmatic attack. He explained that the faster he drove the woman would say "Faster teacher faster." On another occasion he told my mom that he was compelled to drive extremely fast that night because a woman was about to give birth in his car, which he did not want to happen. Incidentally, at his funeral service, Pastor Alleyene who was the presiding pastor, informed everyone that his wife

Sister Alleyene was the baby who was "almost born" in my dad's car that night, many many years ago.

Some parts of the road from Plymouth to Scarborough were absolutely treacherous. The road was built on the edge of a mountain; on one side was the mountain, and on the other side was a precipice. This stretch of road spanned about one mile: It was narrow, and there were no streetlights since it was located between villages. In those days that road was appropriately referred to as "Bad Hill." Today, that road no longer exists. A new road was cut in another area away from the cliffs. To this day it amazes me to no end, to understand how it was possible for my dad to navigate that stretch of road, at the speed he was required to drive, during the night, with any degree of safety.

We thought our dad was the best and most capable dad in the world. He exhibited much competence and confidence always and was adept at everything he did. He once did something which as a little girl, I thought was so remarkable, that I remember the incident clearly up to this day. One night my four sisters and I were accompanying him to our grandparents' home a short distance away. It was somewhat dark because the streetlights were not very effective. We soon encountered a group of people walking towards us. There was crying and loud talking so we knew that something was wrong. When my dad enquired what was the matter, the father explained that his daughter was playing with the sewing machine, and the needle went right through her fingernail and broke off in her finger. They were on their way to the doctor's home. My dad then took the child's hand and with his teeth he quickly extracted the broken needle from her fingernail. That swift action of his de-escalated the confusion and anxiety that night. As a kid I was just simply mesmerized at what he did. I wondered how was it that he always knew what was the appropriate thing to do.

As an educator he excelled; both his speech and his written words were excellent. When he spoke to us, his children, he never diluted his language. My mom as his wife and our mother was the stable force that made our house a home and our family a unit of love. As we grew up the family structure was tight. Our home was characterized by laughter, song and good humour. It was a warm and secure environment which our parents provided, and we five girls grew up happy and without a care in the world. We laughed at everything and everyone. We sometimes got into trouble which necessitated disciplinary action to be administered either by my dad or my mom. We would all cry in sympathy when any one of us got flogged. Flogging your children with a belt was an appropriate way to discipline them in those days.

A huge ship had anchored off the coast of the Plymouth shores. I was only eight years old so I am unable to say what caused this decision to anchor; in retrospect it could have been some type of mechanical engine failure. My dad who was the principal of the Bethesda Government School at that time, decided to take the senior children on a field trip to visit this ship, an educational experience so to speak. Those kids were about twelve years old, but he decided to take me along for the excursion. I remember all of us kids being loaded into two speed boats which transported us way out into the ocean where the big ship was anchored. We were taken aboard and escorted around the big ship by the captain. At one point everyone was crowded around the captain who was demonstrating something or the other to us. Being younger than the other kids, I soon got bored and without anyone being aware, I began wandering away on my own. I must have wandered into a restricted unauthorized area because I can remember the scenario very clearly up to this day: I suddenly found myself in the bow area of the ship, and directly in front of me was a large hole in the ship's floor approximately about six feet in diameter, with a massive chain which I later realized was the anchor, stretching down into the deep blue sea below. Reader, there was a strong possibility I could have fallen into that big hole, and no one would have known what had become of me, I was very close to it. Unspeakable fear gripped me; I turned around and hurried back to the group and never left their side for the rest of the tour. I was so trauma-tized that I did not mention it to anyone. My thoughts of sympathy were usually for my dad. What if I had fallen into that hole, what if when they were ready to return to the boats he found out that I was missing. I shudder to think of his grief, because I know he loved me dearly. But God is good, He kept me from danger. To this day as I think of what could have happened, I cringe.

During our school years my sisters and I always defended and stuck up for each other. Anyone who had a problem with one sister, soon realized that they had a problem with all five of us. What we did, was discuss the issue at home, then our eldest sister Val would come to the conclusion that we give that person the cold shoulder. We lived the old adage; one for all and all for one.

Two

It was the summer of 1960. There was talk in the air that my dad would be transferred back to Trinidad. As a schoolteacher he had been transferred a few times prior, between Trinidad and Tobago. Some of my sisters were born in Tobago and some of us were born in Trinidad. This talk of a transfer to Trinidad was exciting news to us kids, because Trinidad which is a sister island to Tobago is bigger and more appealing, and as far as we knew, there was more excitement taking place there. As teenagers, this opportunity presented a bigger and more interesting world for us to explore, and this prospect made us quite happy and full of anticipation.

Our parents were not at home when the official letter of transfer arrived from the Department of Education that Saturday morning. My older sister Vestine took the liberty of opening the mail, and we were all overjoyed to greet them with the good news when their car drove up into the driveway. "We're going to Matura, Trinidad."

My very last recollection of Plymouth, Tobago at the age of fourteen, is that of the entire family in the green consul driving away from the ancestral home; and looking back to see my grandpa standing in the yard leaning on his cane, crying. One of my sisters reported, "Grandpa is crying." Neither of my parents responded. A few months later we received a telegram that he had passed away. I guess my grandpa had cried because he somehow knew that he would never see his son or his family again.

We received the death message via telegram. It was at a time when we were just settling into our new home in Trinidad. My dad was outside in the yard doing some type of man-duties. We all went outside to deliver the news to him. His response initially was quite brave. "This is news I expected sooner or later," he said. He then continued to speak a few other sentences along that vein. We all thought that our dad was handling the news in stride like he handled everything else. To our astonishment he suddenly broke down in heart-wrenching sobs, while saying, "Lena (my mom), please tell me what to do." We never saw our dad cry before, and we all started crying in sympathy.

My mom then rose to the occasion! I remember her telling him that he must inform the vice-principal Mr. Jack that he will be away from school for the next week. She advised him to get ready to fly over to Tobago the following day. Later that day, she gives him a sum of money to cover his passage and expenses for the trip. She then says, "Here is money to bury your father." He looked at her with surprise as though he wanted to ask, "Where did you get all this money from?" But I am quite sure he knew. You see my dad always turned over his entire paycheque to my mom at the end of the month, and she managed the household finances. She held the purse strings and was shrewd enough to put some money away for emergencies.

Less than a year later we got word that his mother had passed. It was really a sad time for him when he had to return to Tobago a second time, to bury his mother. My maternal grandparents had passed away many years previously, when we were all quite young.

By September 1960, we settled down to life in Trinidad. Sangre Grande was the nearest town and my sister Vestine and I began attending the St. Catherine's Girls' High School there. One Sunday afternoon, a newly made friend of my parents who lived in Sangre Grande was celebrating his birthday and our family was invited. I can clearly remember the yellow dress I wore as I stood before my bedroom mirror, twisting my hair into a Lana Turner style as was the fashion at that time. I had no idea that night would shape my entire life and future.

Our host Mr. Ashby had a daughter by the name of Sylvia. Her boyfriend whose name was Richard attended the party and he brought along his best friend Glasgow as he was called then. I remember sitting in the living room with my family and all the other guests when the two boys walked by. We attached no importance to it, never gave them a second thought.

The following day after school, as we waited for our dad to collect us, the same two boys approached us on their bicycles. My eldest sister asked them what was their mission. Richard stated that Glasgow saw us last night at the party and liked one of the girls. He wanted to be introduced to us. My sister then asked why did Glasgow not speak for himself.

Life in Matura was different. It did not present the glitz and the glamour we had anticipated experiencing in Trinidad, but we tried to make the best of it because, like it or not this was now our home. The school principal's quarters was located on the same grounds as the school; a few short yards away. It was adequate: A spacious house with four large bedrooms; two bedrooms on either side of a huge living room. Behind the living room was a large dining room and adjacent to the dining room was the kitchen which overlooked the school. It was so close that if we spoke too loudly while in the kitchen, our voices would be heard in the school room beneath us.

There was also a long rectangular porch at the front facing the main road which spanned the width of the house. Beside it was a sewing room. This area was enmeshed in mosquito proofing wire. The house was well equipped with screen doors which slammed shut behind you. It was intended I imagine, to keep the mosquitoes out at all costs.

Unfortunately, there were no bathrooms in the house, and we had to use the bathrooms which were provided for the teaching staff and school children. The bathrooms consisted of a row of about ten flushable toilets, two of which were designated for staff. Dad instructed us to use the staff toilets and they were always kept clean by the school janitor Mr. Findley who lived obliquely opposite the school. This was an inconvenience but not really a problem for us as such. Regrettably, the shower was located outdoors. To access it, one had to exit through the bedroom that I shared with my younger sister Allison. It was securely enclosed by sheets of galvanize which afforded us privacy but did not protect us from intruders like snakes. I oftentimes heard my mom complaining to the education officials that one day as my sister Vestine was heading into the shower there was a snake leaving. In retrospect, I think that snake incident was the big reason that caused us to leave Matura as soon as we did.

It was delightful having the entire school-yard property as our playground, when we returned home from school on afternoons. There was an abundance of water from the rows of taps that lined the east side of the school. I remember my dad using the school yard to teach my eldest sister Val to drive the consul.

Sunday afternoons were delightful. We would get dressed up and stand at the front gate where we would have full view of the never-ending streams of cars, as families drove back to Sangre Grande after visiting the beaches of Salibya Bay, which was located about four miles further up north.

We often swam in the crystal-clear river which was located a mere five minutes' walk from home and enjoyed the concerts and other activities that the Matura community had to offer. We enjoyed the kind hospitality of the wonderful people who welcomed us with open arms, and just loved to visit our home.

However, after a year had passed, we realized that we had enjoyed all that there was to enjoy in Matura, but it failed to provide much stimulation for us young people ranging in ages from ten to eighteen years. My dad then decided that we would relocate to the major city of Sangre Grande.

In those days we were not allowed to date, so nothing materialized with our new friend Glasgow, except that he soon became a friend of the entire family. On occasions he would ask permission from my dad to invite us all to different events. On one occasion, I clearly remember all five of us girls accompanied by Glasgow, walking down to the Ascot Cinema to see the movie "Muscle Beach Party" starring Frankie Avalon and Annette Funicello. Of course, my dad had no objections, because he was completely unaware that this young man had an interest in any one particular daughter. He just thought that he was a friend of the girls. Little did he know that as we got older, Glasgow would park his bicycle at our home and then travel down to Port of Spain to meet me after Polytechnic classes so that we could travel up together in a taxi. He would then arrive at our home a little later after the taxi dropped me off, to collect his bike, and pretend that he was just visiting us for the first time that day.

Life in Sangre Grande was the best. Sometimes I find it difficult to come to grips with the fact that we spent only three and a half years there. As my sisters and I used to reminisce; we were all in agreement that those were the best years of our lives.

Our dad rented the upstairs of a huge two-story house overlooking the Eastern Main Road. There were four large bedrooms and a spacious verandah at the front where we spent most of our leisure time, and soon got to know everyone who passed by. As people walked by on the pavement beneath, we would judge who had good fashion sense and who did not. We decided which boys were cute and tried to determine who was dating whom. We totally enjoyed being in the thick of things. I recall the living room and dining room were so spacious that on two occasions we hosted parties, which everyone enjoyed. We made lots of friends who were always dropping in for a visit; there was never a dull moment. It was a time when we as teenagers were happy, devoid of problems, full of energy, and eager to embrace life and enjoy it to the fullest. In essence, a whole new world had opened up for us and we made the most of every moment of each day.

After school our friends would visit our home as we all walked home together. We always were happy to refresh them with cold drinks before they made their way to their own homes. There was an incident that took place when we were attending high school which I had completely forgotten, until my nephew Sean made mention of it in his mother's and my sister Vestine's eulogy in September 2007. But first, allow me to say a few words about my sister Vestine. Throughout our high school years, we both attended the same high schools together. The Trinidad educational system was patterned after the British education system; where the climax of our high school experience should result in our successful mastery of the Senior Cambridge Examination which was set in England. My sister Vestine was an extremely popular and likeable personality, tall and slim with long black hair, and she was full of fun. Apart from that she was academically brilliant, but she did not care to study. To use my dad's terminology, she did not "apply herself to her books," she just loved to play. She had no interest in sitting around the table at night like the rest of us, to study and do our homework.

Since we were attending a Catholic school, it was imperative that we registered for religious studies. Sometimes we would be given an entire chapter of the gospel to memorize verbatim. I would study diligently for hours, sometimes I would set my alarm clock for 3:00 in the morning to study further, to ensure that I knew my work.

Vestine would be outdoors having fun and would later come indoors, take up the Bible, read over the chapter once and was ready for school the next day. As mentioned prior, I was good at mass memorization and was able to get top marks for that subject. We had the same teacher for religious studies and the school being an open-air construct, I was able to hear my sister in her class speaking to the teacher. "But Miss Tam, I can give you the substance of the passage" to which Miss Tam replied, "Vestine I do not want you to give me the substance, I would like you to memorize the passage of scripture like I asked you to." At one point I remember our dad saying to her when she would not settle down to study her schoolwork. "It's okay darling, I will send you to school until those two long black braids on your back turn grey."

She was naturally brilliant in math. I remember dad working with her on math problems. I once heard him presenting to her a scenario in which he stated: A vehicle leaves point A at a certain time, travelling at 45 miles per hour; simultaneously another vehicle leaves point B travelling toward the first vehicle at 35 miles per hour, he wanted her to tell him at what time do they both meet at point C or something like that. That question to me was gibberish; I had no idea how to even begin to solve a problem of that nature, but she was good at math and always nailed the correct answer. That is the reason why my dad pressed her to study because he knew she was capable. As an educator he was very analytical, he knew my brain could not handle that type of math, so he did not even attempt to bother me with a question of that nature, I opted for Art classes.

He was always interested in what we were working on whenever we gathered around the table at night to study, so he would sit in to assist us. When we started high school however, we would all inform him that we were studying a foreign language such as Latin, Spanish or French, to make sure he left us alone. We were aware that in his day, foreign languages were not taught, and that he had no knowledge of such subjects. It was like "good-bye dad, sorry but your assistance is not required here." He used to say that I would do well because I had "stick-to-it-ivness," a word he coined to describe my work ethic. In reality, I was a child who always stuck with a project until completion; I never gave up regardless of how difficult the task was. (Mathematics excluded)

Going back to the incident at school: In late 1961 the St Catherine's High School was taken over and run solely by Nuns. A new Nun had joined the crew at our school; and I believe she did not like me. I always sat at the front of the classroom; that was my seat of choice. This particular day she asked me to give up my seat at the front and had me switch seats with another girl who sat at the back of the class. I complied, thinking that she just wanted the girl to sit up front that day for some unknown reason.

The following morning, both the girl and I resumed our regular seats. The Nun comes into the class to commence her teaching. She quickly realized that I was back in my seat at the front of the class. She roughed me up verbally and told me that seat at the front no longer belonged to me; and that it was a permanent arrangement for the girl to take my seat. I felt hurt because I knew that I was being treated unfairly. I went to the assigned seat and started crying aloud in the class because I felt wronged. I was hurt, and just wanted to give vent to my feelings. At this point, the Nun could not resume teaching her class because I was crying loudly and would not be comforted. My sister Vestine's class was in an adjacent room. I am not sure how she found out what was the matter with me, but she too began crying loudly from her classroom as well. I guess the Nun is now in a quandary, "raucous in the school" as students described it. She probably did some quick calculation: The child in her class whom she had wronged and who is crying aloud, her name is Eslyn Grant; and the other student crying aloud in the other class is Vestine Grant, they must be sisters!!! I am sure she did not want the principal Nun Sister Laurentina to hear the commotion and come across to ask what was happening, because everyone knew that Vestine was a favourite of Sister Laurentina since she was her star pupil. The Nun immediately reversed her decision and called me back to my seat and did not bother me again. All the girls at the school thought that was hilarious, and for the next week that incident was the hot topic of conversation for everyone.

In 1961 television made its appearance in Trinidad. From the moment that they hit the Sangre Grande market; dad purchased one for us. Lots of friends would visit our home to watch television shows with us. Friday nights were exceptional; that's when everyone came to watch the favourite show of all time namely; Bonanza, with the captivating young star "Little-Joe Cartwright." (Michael Landon)

Three

My mom always told me that I had my first asthmatic attack at the age of five. She said it was quite a frightening experience for the whole family. They all thought I would not survive the night. For the following twenty years of my life, I suffered from asthma. I could recall whenever I had an attack it would last about three days. At the end of each bout of illness I would be left feeling weak and tired. As a young child, when I recovered, I would take advantage of the opportunity to request certain favourite treats such as Cannings ice cream and Cadbury's milk chocolate which my dad would always provide for me. I think they all agonized over my condition and out of sympathy, gave me anything I asked for. I recall my maternal grandmother boiling up all types of bush tea for me to drink. Also bottles and bottles of a brown disgusting-tasting concoction which my mom's friend who lived in the village of Buccoo would prepare for me. All these potions were given to me in the hopes of curing my asthma, but the illness persisted.

On one occasion, our friend Glasgow who would usually visit the home was concerned that for so many days I was reportedly sick in bed. I remember my sister Allison telling me, "Your Glasgow says he will be happy just to see your face." I do not think he was aware of my illness and that I was in no position to get out of bed and show my face to anyone. Apparently, he was very concerned about me: The third day as I lay sick in bed, at about 2:00 p.m. that afternoon, my mom and I were alone at home, and I heard his voice. "Good afternoon Mrs. Grant I came to see Eslyn." I could detect the fear in his voice because he was not sure how my mom would react to his coming to the home to visit me; besides, he should be in school at that time. He later told me, he could stay away no longer, he just had to come to visit me, no matter what the cost. It made me realize at that moment that he really cared for me and determined (like Queen Esther) even though he might get into trouble, he was not about to let another day go by without seeing me.

My mom who had previously moved me up to the front bedroom closer to the kitchen so that she could keep an eye on me, came to my room and advised that Glasgow was in the living room and wanted to visit me. She wanted to know if that was okay with me. Of course, I answered in the affirmative. My heart went out to him at that moment, because I knew that it took a lot of nerve on his part to climb up those steps and to ask my mom if he could visit with me.

I remember her bringing a chair from the dining room into the bedroom, and then invited him into my room then she left us. We chatted for a while, I recall him asking how I was feeling, then I believe I fell asleep shortly after, because when I awoke two hours later, he was gone. I think my mom must have told him the nature of my illness; I recall him being quite concerned and protective of me after that.

As a result of those experiences, I am always sympathetic to anyone who has breathing problems because I have been there and can well relate to the horrors. Many years later when we were older and began working in the city, my sister Allison left her place of employment at the Ministry of Education and Culture to have lunch with me at my office. I worked downtown with the Department of Home Affairs and Personnel at that time. I had just recovered from a nasty asthma attack, and this was my first day back to work. After she left to return to her office, a co-worker commented how nice it was of my sister to travel all the way across town to sit and have lunch with me after my illness.

Lots of boys would come to visit our home of course, there were five teenage girls in the house! Everyone sat in the living room and chatted with us under the watchful eyes of my dad who called us his jewels. I once mentioned to my daughter Jacinth who is a therapist, that even though we left Sangre Grande close to sixty years ago, yet sometimes at night when I go to bed and close my eyes, I would envision myself in my bedroom in Sangre Grande. Most times I would have to open my eyes to give myself a reality check regarding the position of the bed in which I now lay. She rightly stated that perhaps the years in Sangre Grande had made such a positive impact on my life, that the subconscious, like an automatic default, reverted back to that joyous season and placed me right in that bed of my youth.

We left Sangre Grande in June 1964. I had completed high school, obtained my General Certificate of Education and was in the market for employment. Apart from gaining employment positions in the private sector, your General Certificate of Education made you eligible to enter the teaching profession or the Civil Service. I was interviewed by officials from the Education Department, and requested a job at my dad's school at Matura Government where there was a vacancy. The interview went well, or so I thought: I went home with my heart full of hope that when schools resumed after the August holidays, I will be travelling alongside my dad to teach with him.

In record time, we made lots of friends in our new home of New Alloville, San Juan, just like we did in Sangre Grande. Everyone was interested in knowing what we were doing with our lives. Well of course my two older sisters were working in Port-of-Spain the capital city, while my two younger sisters were still in high school. I was proud to inform everyone who inquired that I will be teaching at my dad's school in Matura when school resumes after the summer holidays. The weeks in the month of August kept rolling on and I was eager each time the postman rang his bicycle bell to see if there was a letter of appointment for me to begin my teaching job. It was a sad day for me when schools again re-opened and there was no letter of appointment for me from the Department of Education. I know my dad's heart just about broke for me but there was nothing he could do to help me. I needed to be employed by the Department of Education and they sent me no letter of appointment! My eighteenth birthday rolled around, and I secretly hoped that no one would remember it because I felt so inadequate and ashamed of myself. Here I was, about to celebrate my eighteenth birthday with no status: I did not have a job nor was I in school. My self-esteem was at its lowest ebb. I felt unworthy, like I had wasted my life and that I was a failure. On mornings when everyone awoke, the house would be a-buzz with activity; some preparing for school and some for work and I felt so out of place just being at home with my mom who was busy preparing breakfast for her family.

I am sure my mom had no clue of the emotional trauma I was going through, as she would repeatedly request that I go to the shop to purchase food items for her to augment the daily meals, in preparation for the return of the family at the end of the day. I thought it was such a humiliating exercise to be sent to the shop. I would hide in every back lane to and from the store; I did not care for anyone to see me. I cannot recall how long that period of my life lasted, perhaps it was six months or more, but each time she sent me out or called on me to wash up the dishes I felt I would die. I once complained that I was the only one assigned to wash up the dishes, to which one of my sisters responded (I will not say which one) "If you do not want to do the dishes then you should either go to school or go to work." Unfortunately, I was in no position to do either; I was in limbo. I thought this situation would never end and that would be my lot for the rest of my life; I was in such despair. In hindsight, I should have explained to my mother my feelings and how humiliating these shop errands made me feel. I am sure she would have left me alone, but I did not wish to share my shame with anyone. To make matters worse, while walking in the yard one day I encountered the contractor Mr. Cato. I believe he was puttering around the yard, putting on the finishing touches to the lovely four-bedroom house he had just built for us. Even now, I remember him clearly; he walked with a limp as one of his legs was shorter than the other. He said to me, "What are you doing home. Did you not tell me you will be going out to teach in September?" I answered very timidly in the affirmative. He then said to me with a sympathetic look on his face," You got disappointed?" I told him yes. I guess he saw how sad I was because he gave me a valuable lesson. He told me that I should not allow that situation to overwhelm me. Life, he said, is full of disappointments, and that things will work out for me eventually. Those were such kind and encouraging words, they helped to lift my spirit for the rest of that day.

It was a happy day some six months later, when I received a letter in the mail from the Education Department assigning me as Teacher One to the Febeau Government School in San Juan. My dad later found out that the officer who officiated in my former application for employment, deliberately did not appoint me to the Matura post because he had a problem with my dad. In retrospect, that pain was short lived, but to an eighteen-year-old it was nothing but brutal! I remember having bad thoughts about that cruel man, his name was Mr. Morton. From my recollection I remember him being an old man, but in reality, he was probably in his sixties. In my mind I would conjure up scenarios in which he would be on his death bed, and I would have the opportunity to sneak into his hospital room, where I would tell him of the distress he had caused me; tell him how wicked and cruel I thought he was, and that I wished he would burn in hell!

Four

In 1965 Glasgow left Trinidad to study in England; he made a promise to me that he will be back in three years after completing his studies and we would get married. I had taught for a while, then I began working with the Department of Home Affairs and Personnel. True to his word Joe returned in early 1969 and we became engaged to be married in July of the following year. During that visit I recalled my fiancé Joe asking me to accompany him to the beach. Of course, I had to ask my dad's permission. I was astounded when he objected to this request! I thought he was being very unreasonable: Joe, my fiancé, had only two weeks' vacation in Trinidad, the next time we would see each other the following year would be to get married, and yet he had a problem with us going to the beach alone, during the day. When I pressed him, he consented, but with the condition that my older sister Vestine should accompany us. I then argued that I was twenty-two years of age, and I did not understand why he needed to have my sister accompany us. He responded, "When Joe goes back to England, I would not know where to find him." I was so annoyed at that remark, that I just ended the conversation. Unaware of all that was taking place, Joe shows up the following morning decked out in beach apparel with camera, all ready to roll. I guess my mom felt sorry for us, knowing how disappointed he would have been, so she gave us permission to go on our own even though my sister was unable to accompany us. We had a nice time at the beach and returned before my dad arrived home from work. My mom never told him that she had to over-ride his unreasonable objection to our date.

On his return to England in 1969, Joe grasped the opportunity to migrate to Canada, where he was offered a permanent position in Portage La Prairie, Manitoba as a Vocation Rehabilitation Counsellor. I oftentimes applaud him for deciding to move to Canada. At this point I will just pause to acknowledge the blessing of living in such a country as ours.

Joe arrived in Trinidad in early July 1970, one week prior to our wedding. It was such a happy time for us all, our parents, siblings and our friends enjoying the occasion. The reception took place at my parents' home as was the custom in those days. At 11:00 p.m. we left for our honeymoon at ChagaCabana Guest House in Chagaramus. My dad and mom were driving us there along with my two-year-old nephew Sean. The party at the house was in full swing with everyone eating and drinking and dancing and having a good time while we slipped away. Sitting in the back seat with my new husband, we were all talking and discussing the events of the day. It was our intention to spend a few days honeymooning before leaving to return to Canada, since Joe had just started his new job and was only allowed two weeks' vacation.

What I was not aware of at that time is that Joe had actually signed himself out of the hospital in Portage La Prairie to get on the plane to be at the wedding. Six weeks earlier he had gone for a swim at Delta beach in the month of May and had developed a severe case of pneumonia. The doctor refused to sign him out because he believed he was too sick to leave the hospital. Joe however informed him that he was getting out of the hospital even if he had to sign himself out, which he did. Thanks be to God, by the time he arrived in Trinidad to get married he was okay; no one had a clue that he was so extremely sick a few weeks prior.

As mentioned previously, my dad has always been an exceptionally good driver. To this day I am not sure what happened but there was a collision on Wrightson Road with another vehicle at a roundabout on our way to our honeymoon. The collision was so severe that it forced our vehicle off the road and unto the median; our vehicle was completely out of control at that point. As I remember we were going at a high speed, heading towards a huge light pole, and I thought for sure we were all going to die. My dad however was determined that was not going to happen under his watch. I saw him fighting with the steering wheel with all his might, to take control of the car, which he eventually did.

My dad and my brand-new husband immediately exited the vehicle to survey the damage. You could imagine my consternation when my mom suggested that we return home for the night and postpone the honeymoon until the following day. I instantly began to panic at this suggestion. I had no intention of inviting my new husband into my bedroom that night, because I would be embarrassed to face my parents the next morning. All sorts of thoughts were swirling around in my mind. I thought that Joe will have to sleep on the couch, or we could drop him off at his dad's home if indeed we had to return home that night.

As we sat there, Pastor Turnell Nelson who had married us a few hours earlier happened to be driving along Wrightson Road and stopped. I remember him sitting in the driver's seat of our car and said a prayer of thanks to the Lord for saving us. He remarked, "You all could have made headlines in tomorrow's papers. Couple married today and killed on the way to their honeymoon."

Before long we were surrounded by about a dozen familiar faces; guests who were at the wedding reception! We were all surprised to see them, but unknown to us, after Joe had surveyed the damage to our car and determined it was inoperable, he went across the street to one of the houses where he made a phone call home. My sister Allison later told me that as soon as the news of the accident was received, the partying ended, and quite a few of the guests decided to come to our aid. Before I realized what was happening, Joe and I were escorted to another vehicle along with our bags and whisked away to our honeymoon. I guess my mom was not happy about that because she thought it was too late for us to continue on to our honeymoon destination. I however was as "pleased as punch" to escape her suggestion of returning home that night.

Because of Joe's quick thinking that night in phoning home, my dad became very impressed with my husband, and since that incident he has always called him a "man of action." I remember him saying that Joe could never live in a house in which doors or windows were falling apart. He described him as being constantly "on the ball" since he always did immediately whatever needed to be done. For the record, I would like to mention at this point, that my husband Joe is still very much the "man of action" as my dad so aptly described him some fifty years ago.

Five

One week later we left Trinidad for Canada, where a new and beautifully furnished apartment awaited me in Portage La Prairie. Life in Canada was so different for me; it was bittersweet. I missed my family an awful lot, but at the same time I began to enjoy my new life with my new husband.

We arrived in Portage La Prairie in the month of July 1970, and I was fascinated by the fact that the sun remained high up in the sky at 9:30 in the evening. Also, my first experience with the snow was interesting. In the Caribbean I always admired the Christmas cards with the sparkling snow on the Christmas trees and now here I was actually seeing it. The first winter however presented quite a challenge for me. I could not understand why I kept falling whenever I went outdoors. It took me almost a week before I discovered that I needed winter boots, which were specifically made with special soles, to facilitate walking on ice during the winter months. The golden leaves on the trees that kept falling during the autumn months, was also a pleasant sight for me. All that I read and saw in books and cards now became a reality, that was amazing!

In September of that year, we left Portage La Prairie to attend the Assiniboine College in Brandon. It was a strange feeling being the only black female student in the entire college. I became very self-conscious and felt that everyone was looking at me. Some students wanted to touch my hair and others looked at my fingernails and were surprised that they were not black as the rest of my skin. My accent also fascinated them; they asked me silly questions just to hear me respond. They thought my accent was cute. To all this I would respond "What accent?" I did not believe I had an accent; they were the ones with the accent, not me!

I really flirted with danger during that first winter. Somehow the cold weather did not seem to affect me that much, so I thought I would just ignore it. I would sometimes run from the apartment to the car without a coat, and when I did wear one, I did not even bother to bundle myself up warmly. That was so unwise because at the end of the winter I developed a severe case of pneumonia. Initially, I believed it to be an asthmatic attack; but in hindsight I should have been hospitalized in the spring of 1972. Breathing for me was extremely difficult, it was an awful experience. I suffered for months and was unable to sleep at night. I was down to 90 pounds from my usual 115 pounds. At that point I began praying to God for help, but my spiritual resources were limited. As a child, on Sundays we attended church as a family, we sang hymns, we listened to Bible readings. My dad was a lay preacher at times; but after church services we would return home not giving much thought to what was said. We were taught to kneel and say our prayers at night, on mornings, and also before meals; but we had no understanding of what it meant to have a personal relationship with the living God.

Praise God, who is merciful to all, in the summer of 1972 my health began to mend. I recall I was so excited to report to my husband one evening, that I was able to actually run to get the bus to go to work that day. Prior to that day, it took so much effort even to walk. I worked at the Attorney General's office on Taylor Ave, and there is where I first met my friend Gracita Jones while we both waited for our husbands to take us home after work. To this day I do not know why my supervisor did not fire me from the job, because at work I coughed constantly. One might ask why did you not just stay at home? But having to rise on mornings, get ready for work and leave the house was therapy for me. I felt so much better going out; there was a feeling of suffocation just being within those four walls at home. I could never forget the beautiful group of people with whom I worked. Despite my annoying cough they were so kind to me; Nellie, Pat, Brenda, Ingrid and many more whose names I cannot recall, but that was almost fifty years ago. As the summer months rolled on, I began to feel so much better, and I was really happy to feel normal again.

One Sunday morning my husband and I were at a gas station in St. James close to where we lived, when I noticed this family with their Bible in hand on their way to church. Immediately that touched a soft place in my heart. I suddenly experienced a sense of guilt as I realized that the Lord did not play much of a role in my life. I did in fact spend a few moments on mornings and again a few moments at nights saying prayers but beyond that I had no connection with, nor felt any need for Him in my life. That encounter with that family was the beginning of my hunger and thirst for the Lord. I began to feel a yearning for Him, I felt a void in my heart, something was missing! What I did not know at that time is that the Lord has made mankind with a need for Him and that void, that feeling of emptiness, can only be filled by Him, the Creator.

One Sunday, I attended a little church on Isbister Street close to my house. This happened to be an all-white congregation and the members appeared to be annoyed that I was there. No one greeted me or spoke to me. When I later mentioned this incident to my friend Barbara who lived close by, she informed me that she had a similar experience in that church. She sat in a pew in which a man was sitting, and he never stopped moving till he was in another pew completely. I never went back to that church, but the deep-seated need for the Lord was still there in my heart.

One blessed day I returned home from work, as my husband was leaving to go out on an errand. After chatting for a while, he nonchalantly told me, "Your mother and your sister (Allison) wrote you a letter, you are sure to become a Christian after you've read it." Little did he know how prophetic his words were. As soon as he left, I sat down and I read the letter in its entirety. They informed me that they had found a Saviour and that they wanted to introduce Him to me. His name is Jesus, He has washed away their sins and now the entire household is living for Him. When I got through reading that letter, I just wanted to experience this Jesus for myself. I knelt beside my dining room table at 29 Downs Avenue in St. James and just gave my heart to the Lord. I did in fact pray the "Sinner's Prayer" even though at that time, I did not know that is what it was called. I invited Him into my heart, I asked Him to forgive my sins, wash me in His blood and save me, I know that the Holy Spirit helped me to pray that prayer. I cannot recall how long I stayed on my knees, but when I ended my prayer, I became fully aware that a spiritual transaction had taken place. I knew I had passed from spiritual death to spiritual life; there was an inner change of my heart. I knew I was "born again." Some people take illicit drugs to get high; I can tell you that I experienced a spiritual high that made me feel like I was walking on "Cloud 9." In addition to that feeling, I experienced an unspeakable and indescribable joy in my heart, and I just knew it was the joy of salvation.

At that moment I realized I needed to start attending a church. I had been listening to "Faith to Live By" services with pastor H.H. Barber on the television, and I remembered him inviting listeners to attend services at Calvary Temple Church which according to him was "located in the heart of downtown Winnipeg."

I worked downtown at Pioneer Grain in the Richardson Building, so after work the following day, which was a Friday, I walked to the church, where I met Mrs. Barber for the first time; a very lovely Christian woman. I told her about my experience with the Lord. She was very warm, welcoming, and listened intently to what I had to say, then arranged for me to speak with the pastor on Sunday morning prior to the service. I remember her saying to him as she introduced me, "This is the young lady I was telling you about." Pastor Barber was interested in hearing my testimony, he encouraged me in the Lord, ministered to me for a while, then directed me to attend the Convert's Class. Thus began my fellowship at Calvary Temple Church where I worshipped for the next thirty years under his ministry.

A few months after I had given my heart to the Lord, I noticed that the asthmatic attacks had ceased. As I grew in the Lord, I came to learn that when the Lord saves you, He not only takes care of the sin problem and forgives your sins, but He also makes you completely whole. It has been fifty years now and I have never suffered another asthma attack. The scripture says; "If the Son therefore shall make you free, you shall be free indeed" **John 8:36.**

After I invited the Lord into my heart, I realized that all my fears and uncertainties were turned into confidence, and that there was a renewal of my outlook in every aspect of my life. I had that wonderful assurance that my future would be good, because of the continual dwelling of His presence within my heart. I also felt led to read the book of Ephesians; how I enjoyed reading that book, and it ministered to me powerfully during the first few months of my walk with God.

Six

About a month or so later I realized I was pregnant with my first child. Words fail me to express the level of my joy when my baby was placed in my arms for the first time. I can still envision my husband's wide grin from ear to ear when the nurse wheeled us out from the delivery room, and he laid eyes on his baby for the first time. The baby himself was absolutely beautiful. We were surprised that his complexion was so light. Most of the nurses looked puzzled when they saw my husband. We took baby Justin home and life was never the same for us after that. For me I could not believe this perfect little being was formed in my body. There he was with curly black hair, black eyes and pink lips. I would just gaze at him for hours as he slept, and felt so good that he was totally dependent on me; if I did not change his clothes they would not be changed, if I did not feed him, he would not be fed. I relished the fact that he was completely dependent on me, and I totally enjoyed mothering this little person whom the Lord had entrusted into my care. From that moment I decided I would not be going back to work, I preferred to stay at home and take care of my baby. The only drawback was that I had to explain to everyone who inquired, why his complexion was so light. I was not sure how to answer their questions, so I would oftentimes try to explain that it was probably a throwback to my parents whose ancestry were white, and they were very light in complexion. To make matters worse my husband came home from work one evening very unhappy: A friend of his namely Eddie Price, who worked with him at the Headingly Prison, told the guys at work that Joe had a white baby, and they began to tease him. They thought it was hilarious that he had a white baby and both him and his wife were black people.

One day while at church someone came up to me and asked the same question. "Why does he look so white?" There I was again, trying to explain the reason for his complexion, when an older Christian woman who was nearby answered for me. Her response was as follows, "That's the way the Lord made him." I was so very grateful for her wise intervention, and from that moment onwards, that was the perfect answer I gave to everyone who asked. Needless to say, that answer ended all questions or conversation about his complexion. When our last child Shelley was born, her complexion was as light as our first baby. The morning my husband Joe arrived at the hospital to take us home, a nurse whom I never saw before was on duty that morning. She simply refused to release the baby to us, even though the name on the beaded necklace on my daughter spelled out my name, matching the name-band on my wrist. As she disappeared back into the nursery for clarification my husband sat down on the bed beside me and said, "Well, let's just sit here and wait to see how long it will take her, before she returns and gives our baby to us."

By 1977 our family had grown to five in number, and I was the happiest woman alive. I thoroughly enjoyed taking care of my three children; Justin, Jacinth and Shelley. I vowed to be the best parent I could be and determined to take care of all their needs in every area of their lives; the physical, spiritual, emotional, educational, and social well-being.

I clearly remember on Sunday afternoons at a certain season in our lives, we would all crowd into the family room along with dad to watch "The Wonderful World of Disney." I took them to church on Sunday mornings at Calvary Temple, and made sure they knew that we all as individuals needed to have a relationship with the Lord.

Over the years since my salvation experience, the Lord has been very good to me, and I had always shared those experiences with the kids. One morning I had completed a reading form for each child to take to school. During that month, there was a special reading promotion for each grade. All the kids were supposed to read for twenty minutes each day. I religiously worked with them on that project. At the end of the month, they were supposed to return the reading log to the teacher where they could be recognized for their reading exercises. That particular Friday morning, I completed each child's sheet, signed it, placed it in their school bags, and they were off to school to deliver it to their teachers, where they expected to be congratulated for having completed the exercise. Shortly after the kids left home the Holy Spirit spoke to me. His Spirit spoke to my spirit telling me that I had made a big mistake. Look at the calendar, He said. It is now the 23rd of the month but you thought it was 30th. You have signed up the kids' forms as though they read for the entire month and there is still another week to go before the month is over. Should the kids take those forms to school you will be opening yourself to ridicule, they might even think you are a liar. I immediately dropped what I was doing and as fast as a bolt of lightning I was out the door. I soon overtook the kids, removed the reading log from their book bags and returned home. As I opened the forms, exactly like the Holy Spirit had warned me; I had completed the form and given the kids credit for reading assignments which had not even been done. Had those kids taken those forms to school; I would have been the butt of jokes among those teachers at school, that would have been so shameful for me. However, in His word the Lord has promised to keep us from shame. "And my people shall never be ashamed." **Joel 2:26.** That is what He did for me that day. I was able to hold on to the logs until the following Friday when it was due, and duly had the kids complete their reading assignment.

As the kids grew, we had a lot of fun. I was the chief disciplinarian in the home. Dad went out to work and I stayed at home to take care of business, since we did not like the idea of babysitters raising our kids. I was a stay-at-home mom for ten years until our last child went out to school; it was at that time that I decided to become enrolled at the University of Manitoba to pursue my Bachelor of Arts Degree.

During my time at home, whenever a problem arose with the kids and I felt I needed his support, I would call in the "big guns" namely dad; to help with discipline. The evening in question I asked dad to speak to the kids to enforce the rules, whatever the problem was, I cannot recall at this time. Justin was about twelve years of age, Jacinth ten, and Shelley eight. It was about 8 p.m. that evening when dad called everyone around his bed. He began by addressing Shelley. He told her that her showers were too long and that she was wasting water. He then addressed Jacinth by telling her that it is time she got a job and started paying taxes. At this time, we are all confused because his eyes are wide open, and he is speaking very forcefully. He then turned to Justin and accused him of running away to British Columbia to hide from the police. At that point we all realized that despite the fact that his eyes were open he was fast asleep and perhaps thought he was speaking to a client. Dad at that time was employed as a Mental Health Specialist with the Provincial government. I then had to shake him out of his stupor and inquired what nonsense was he telling the kids. Laughter erupted around the bed. Needless to say, that was the end of his input for a long time.

In the early 1980's some friends of ours introduced us to camping. For the next seven years our family travelled all over North America in our faithful motor home. From the moment school was through at the end of June, we would take off on our travels. Sometimes we would travel as far west as Victoria, British Columbia or as far south as Disney World in Florida. We loved our motor home, which was cozy, and afforded us all the comforts of home but on a far smaller scale. KOA Kampgrounds of America became our nightly destination when we travelled through The United States. We would usually travel as far as time and finances would allow. On our return trip to Winnipeg, we would do the kids' school shopping for the next school term. Our favourite store for shoes was Payless, where we would purchase sometimes as many as twenty pairs of shoes, since the prices were affordable.

It was also customary as the kids grew older, that we would get together on Sunday afternoons where we would have "talks." If they did anything wrong during the week, I would discuss it with them. Long ago before I even had kids, I decided I would not discipline my kids in the same manner in which my parents, and most other parents from the Caribbean Islands disciplined their children. We spent a lot of time talking things through.

One Saturday afternoon I attended a film show that was sponsored by the West Indian fellowship at Calvary

Temple. The film was entitled "Left Behind." It depicted how the Lord had raptured all who were saved and living for Him and the chaos, confusion and fear that this event caused in the world for those who were left behind. When I returned home, I told the kids about the film. I also related to them how the television anchor person came on the air and wanted to know: "Where is Billy Graham, how could millions of people just disappear!" As I recall, it was a very sobering film. At the conclusion, Pastor Barber who was seated at the rear of the auditorium came to the front and spoke of the necessity of salvation; of accepting the Lord into one's heart. I cannot recall whether he made an altar call that night.

When I shared this film with my children, they all got annoyed with me. Shelley said to me, "How would you feel if you went up to heaven in the rapture and your husband and kids were left behind. How happy would you be then?" They also reminded me, that I told them to ask the Lord to save them which they did, and that nothing was happening. What they did not know is that their mom was already praying ardently to the Lord to save them.

A couple of months later, one Pastor Dennis White from Trinidad held a week-long evangelistic crusade at Calvary Temple. This particular night the kids and I got dressed to attend the meeting. It was a delightful evening; the kids were all in a jovial and happy mood, as we settled into our pews at church. The pastor began to preach, the sermon was captivating even for the children, except Shelley who had taken off her shoes had fallen asleep on my lap. At the end of the service the pastor made an altar call. I did not want to have to tell my kids to go forward; I thought it was a personal decision they needed to make on their own. People started streaming down to the altar. I hoped to see my kids do the same, but they were still beside me. When I looked across at Justin, his eyes were closed, and his lips were moving; he was praying; that inaction of his bewildered me. I said to him, "Don't you want to get saved?" He answered "Yes" emphatically. I then said to him "What are you waiting for, this is not a time to pray, it's a time to go to the altar and accept Jesus like the pastor is calling you to do." I did not have to speak any further to them, they both hastened down to the altar as the pastor was still calling.

All this while Shelley was fast asleep on my lap. I tried to wake her: I pulled at her ear lobe and called her name, but she was sound asleep. I thought I would just leave her alone; she is young, she will have many more opportunities in the future to accept Jesus as Lord and Saviour. I was quite happy that the older siblings were down at the altar. Suddenly Shelley sits upright and said to me, "Where are Justin and Jacinth?" I responded that they went down to the altar to give their hearts to the Lord. She then said, "What about me?" I said, "You can go too if you want to surrender to the Lord." She immediately began hastening to get her feet into her shoes and down she went to the altar. I later joined them at the altar and experienced the joy of their salvation like I did when I was saved. Out of curiosity, I later asked Shelley what made her get up so suddenly, after I was trying everything I possibly could to wake her and was unable to do so. She responded that in her sleep, she heard the voice of the pastor giving the altar call. His voice woke her up, and she wanted to be saved. Well, I was very happy because she in particular was so concerned about the rapture and her salvation, it would have been heart-breaking for her to sleep through it all, and to realize later that she missed it. The scripture says, today is the day of salvation, we should not put it off for tomorrow. "Behold now is the accepted time, behold now is the day of salvation." **2 Corinthians 6:2.**

Alpheus & Henrietta Williams;
my maternal grandparents & family.

Wilfred & Helena Grant; (dad & mom)
Allison, Cilda, Eslyn (front row)
Vestine & Valerie (back row)
1958

Dad & Mom
Vestine, Allison, Cilda, Eslyn, Valerie
1964

Joe & Eslyn's wedding photo.
1970

Family Photos 55

Cilda, Allison, Eslyn, Valerie & Vestine.
1994

Glasgow family photo.
Eslyn, Joe & children
Justin, Shelley & Jacinth
1991

Family Photos 57

Vestine, husband Hamid O'Brien and their children.
1994

Jameson family photo.
Ronald & Allison
Marlon, Cherese & Kevern
1995

Family Photos 59

Joe & Eslyn celebrating their 50th Wedding Anniversary.

Joe & Eslyn surrounded by their children, spouses & grandchildren.
2019

Seven

As the years rolled by, I was able to recognize the Lord's divine intervention in many areas of my life. In the following two chapters, I will share some of these experiences with you.

One night after the kids were in bed, I remained up to do some laundry; however, I began feeling so sleepy that I thought I would just go to bed and finish the laundry the next day. I began climbing the stairs to my bedroom, but my spirit was strongly urging me to finish the laundry. The urging was so strong that I decided to retrieve the last load, before going to bed. I walked downstairs to the laundry room and began removing the clothes from the dryer. At first, I could not understand why the clothes were so very hot, they were burning my arms. As I stood there trying to determine what was happening, to my surprise, black smoke started billowing out from the electrical outlet that the dryer was plugged into. I immediately dropped the bundle of laundry, raced upstairs as fast as I could, got my three children out of their beds, and led them downstairs to the front door. I then instructed them to "stay put" till I came back to get them. With the cell phone in my hand, after dialing my husband who was working nights, I returned to the basement to see what I could do to mitigate the damage that was about to take place. Joe instructed me to unplug the dryer that was still smouldering, which I did. He then directed me to turn off the main electrical switch. I turned it off as he instructed but I was not prepared for what happened next. The phone went dead, and the entire house was plunged into darkness. I silently thanked the lord that the kids were at the front door obediently waiting for me, as I navigated my way out of the dark basement and through the front door. We then went to our neighbour's home who called the fire department. We all knew it was the prompting of the Holy Spirit why I did not just go upstairs and retire to bed. He saved us from perishing in a fire that night.

One morning when all the kids were at school, I was sitting in my family room doing some reading. I felt the urge to move from that position and to step into the kitchen. I however, did not see the need to stop reading and go into the kitchen so I just kept on reading. The urge to leave that room however got stronger and stronger. Because I could not shake that feeling, I reluctantly got up and went as I was led. No sooner had the soles of my feet touched the kitchen floor I heard a loud explosion right where I was sitting. The noise was so very loud that fear paralyzed me for a while. Soon it was time for the kids to come home for lunch. They were all in elementary school at that time. I then told them about the frightening loud explosion that I had just heard; I was even afraid to return to the family room, because I had no idea what had caused the noise.

Justin went outside to investigate and returned with a

bullet from a pellet gun in his hand. Apparently, someone drove by in a car and shot at the glass right above where I was sitting previously. When we examined the triple glass pane, we realized that the bullet was so powerful that it pierced the triple pane and shattered it. Then again, I just knew it was the Holy Spirit who was trying to get me away from the danger that He saw heading my way.

I would now like to share with you another occasion in which the Holy Spirit was able to hide me from shame. I received a credit card in the mail at the end of April (cannot recall the year). I do not particularly like to use credit cards, so I just tucked it away in a safe place and forgot about it. During the summer months I usually prefer to get my exercise by walking outdoors rather than visiting the gym. I always enjoyed the few precious months of summer and sun and liked being outdoors whenever I could. This particular day I noticed in the newspaper that a new Winners store was having its grand opening right in my area. Since I was doing my usual walk, I thought I would visit the store to see if there was anything that I would like to purchase. The most convenient form of cash to take was my credit card so I fished it out, and away I went on my usual routine. When I got to the Winner's store, I followed the crowd and soon found myself sorting through some adorable summer dresses. I selected three dresses, tried them on, was satisfied with the fit and proceeded to the checkout counter. As I handed my credit card to the clerk, I happened to glance behind me. Apparently, this was the only checkout counter that was open, and there was a long line of people behind me with anxious faces awaiting their turn. As the clerk was processing my purchase with my card, a thought popped into my head. What if this card does not work for some reason? This will be super embarrassing for me I thought, particularly since I had no back-up plan, no other money, no purse, just the credit card. I silently prayed that there were no hitches because everyone was staring at me as my transaction was being processed. Another thing that concerned me is that I was the only black person in line, because of this fact I felt super self-conscious. I thought that the shame of being asked to replace the dresses if the card did not work would be unbearable.

Fortunately, everything worked well with the card, and I left the store with my purchase. About three weeks later I decided to go shopping at Sears in St. Vital. When I was about to pay, I thought I would use the card again. This was a purchase made at the lingerie section and I was the sole purchaser at the counter. There was a puzzled look on the face of the cashier as she processed my card. She tried it a few times and seemed confused. I asked what was the problem and she informed me that a code kept popping up which she did not recognize, she had never seen it before. Of course, I had my handbag and was able to pay cash for the item. We chatted for a while and she suggested that I should contact my credit card company when I got home, because she could not determine what was wrong with my card. When I arrived home I phoned the credit card company, I needed an explanation why the card did not work this time. The gentleman on the other end of the phone took my information then he says to me, "Just a minute Mrs. Glasgow, there's a little problem I'll fix it for you right away." After a few moments he returned to the phone then said to me, "You did not activate your credit card before you went shopping, now it is activated, you can go shopping as much as you like." Immediately I thought of the shopping I did at Winners. I then said to him, "I have a question for you, is there any possibility that I could have gone shopping successfully with this card without it being activated?" His answer to me was, "No madam, impossible." I thanked him, hung up the phone, then I began to praise the Lord for what he had done for me at Winners store. It was the same inactivated card that worked for me three weeks ago, because the Lord did not want me to be ashamed in the presence of all those people. "My people shall never be ashamed." **Joel 2: 26-27.** When I related the incident to my sister Val, her response was, "The Lord is God even over technology; the impossible becomes possible when He intervenes." It is noteworthy to mention at this point, that I did receive the statement at the end of the month from the credit card company. The purchases from Winners were recorded. My God is a God of integrity, He did not allow me to have the dresses for free, and He wanted Winners to be paid! Remember the words, "Render unto Caesar the things that are Caesar's." **Mark 12:17.**

One evening in the fall of 2003 I left home to visit my dressmaker who lives in the north end of the city. I live in the south end. I am a person who drives very confidently in areas where I am comfortable and familiar with; if I find myself out of my comfort zone in unfamiliar territory, I become nervous. I believe that is because I do not have a good sense of direction. To get to my destination that evening I knew only one route to go and one route to return; any detours and I'm lost, totally lost. On this day I yielded onto Waverley Street and realized that a blanket of fog had covered everywhere as far as I could see. Visibility was extremely poor; I could hardly see 50 yards ahead of me. Unfortunately, I had already settled myself in the far-left hand lane getting ready to exit unto Bishop Grandin (left) which would take me to Kenaston, where I would begin my long highway ride to the north end. It took me a little while to realize that this was an impossible situation. I began to get worried. The Holy Spirit then spoke to my spirit very clearly, "Turn around and return home." I then said, "But Lord how could I turn around, this is Waverley. To turn around I would have to cross three lanes of traffic to make the loop to Bishop Grandin to get back to my home via Chancellor." Around that time of the evening, Waverley is usually very busy, with traffic in all three lanes. The Spirit of the Lord spoke to me again. He said to me, "Never mind the traffic I have cleared it for you." As I made a quick shoulder-check to the right, just like the Lord said, there was not one vehicle in sight. All the lanes were empty, so I was able to drive right across the three lanes on Waverley and unto Bishop Grandin where I did a loop back around to Chancellor to get home. I wish to explain that whenever I say that the Lord spoke to me and I to him, it is not an audible voice. If you were a passenger in my car, you will hear nothing; His Spirit spoke to my spirit and mine responded. When I got back home about ten minutes later, I phoned the woman to let her know that I would not be able to keep my appointment that evening because of the fog. She said to me, "It's a good thing you did not attempt to come because you cannot see a thing on the highway, it's a complete white-out." I immediately began to thank the Lord for his protection that evening, had I gone that would have been a total disaster, cell phones were not even fashionable at that time. Thank God, again He protected me from a disastrous situation. "I will instruct thee and teach thee in the way which thou shalt go:" **Psalm 32:8.**

My husband and I visited the Caribbean in the spring of 2006. We spent some time in Trinidad and Tobago and then we decided to visit the island of St. Vincent. He had recently been in touch with some relatives who lived there, so he decided it would be nice to visit them. While there we were invited by some friends, Vernice and Vibert Creese to their home for a visit. This couple had recently migrated from Winnipeg and were settling into life in the island. They were very hospitable; they showed us around their lovely home and then decided that we would have a meal together. Since their home is situated in such a vantage area where one can see the beauty of the hillside as the night lights were turned on in the evening, we decided to eat on the porch as opposed to eating indoors at the dining table. Vernice and I both went into the kitchen where she proceeded to put together four plates of food for us to take back to the porch where the men were sitting. I must mention at this point that I am not a person who is great at noting details, I am not very observant; so, I guess I did not bother to note certain particulars about the levels of the floors in the house, which indeed I should have. She prepared the first plate of delicious looking Caribbean style food which I was supposed to take out to my husband then return for mine. I left the kitchen with my husband's plate and proceeded towards the porch where the men were sitting. It was a full plate, so I held it in front of me with both hands. Suddenly the Holy Spirit spoke to me. He told me to stop immediately. He then in a split-second told me a mouthful. He said to me that two feet ahead of me there was a drop in the flooring (a step down to another level in the verandah) and because of the way I was holding the plate and looking across at the men and the beautiful sight in the background, I could not see the almost six-inch drop in the flooring. As I removed one hand and held the plate in the other, what I saw was exactly what the Holy Spirit had told me. I dread to think of what would have happened had the Holy Spirit not intervened; I know it would have been an awful accident.

The two men sat there looking at me as I walked towards them and probably wondered why did I pause for that moment. They had no clue what I was just saved from, and I was too shook up to even say a word to them about my near tragic experience.

Eight

One morning, I awoke from sleep and realized that my lips were swollen almost twice its size. My doctor tried many different medications but to no avail. As a last resort he decided to put me on a regimen of steroid treatments for a week. Each day for seven days he would reduce the number of tablets by one. It worked well for me but at the end of the seventh day when all the tablets were done, the problem flared up again. What compounded the dilemma was that I was due to travel to Trinidad to visit my aging parents the following week. While in Winnipeg, I could always hide at home when this problem persisted, but how could I travel when I looked so unsightly, there was no place to hide! When I phoned the doctor from work and informed him that the moment the steroid medication had ended the problem had flared up again, he reluctantly informed me that there was nothing else he could do for me. He could not keep me on steroids indefinitely it was too dangerous. At that moment I knew what I had to do: I phoned Pastor H. H. Barber from work the very same day. I told him I had a medical problem and I needed spiritual intervention. I requested that he anoint me with oil and pray for me at the Wednesday evening prayer meeting; as the scripture exhorted us to do in the book of **James 5:14** "Is any sick among you? Let him call for the elders of the church; and let them pray over him, anointing him with oil in the name of the Lord."

My expectation was that, at the conclusion of the service the pastor would call me privately and do as I requested; but instead, at the commencement of the service on that Wednesday evening, I panicked as he called me out by name and asked me to come to the front of the church. He then announced that I had requested prayer and anointing for healing, and then invited to the altar all those who needed prayer and anointing for healing as well. Before long, there was a long line of people formed on either side of me spanning the entire width of the altar. Pastor Barber started to pray for each person individually anointing them with oil. Meanwhile at the altar I "meant business" with the Lord, I wanted to be healed, I needed to be healed and I decided in my heart, that I was not going to leave the altar in the same condition as I went up. I reached out to the Lord in faith, I closed my eyes, lifted both hands in surrender and prayed silently. As the pastor began praying for the first person at the beginning of the line, I appropriated for myself, every prayer he uttered. He came down the line, he anointed and prayed for me, and then continued to pray for the other people on the right side of me. When the pastor ceased to pray, I opened my eyes and realized I was the only person remaining at the altar with my hands still outstretched heavenward. I was not aware that as he prayed and anointed everyone, they all returned to their seats. I then quickly returned to my seat somewhat embarrassed, hoping that I did not make too much of a display of myself.

On my arrival in Trinidad the following week, I related to my sister Allison what had happened at the altar. When she heard the part that I was the only person left standing at the altar when I opened my eyes with my hands still outstretched, she erupted into a fit of laughter and laughed heartily to her heart's content. She stated that I had probably made a spectacle of myself and wondered what the people in the congregation thought of me. That was okay, I did not mind her ribbing one bit, whether I made a spectacle of myself or not was of no consequence to me; I was satisfied with the outcome, because I received my healing that night. The Lord had healed me.

My daughter Shelley and her two-year-old son Jacob were visiting me one morning. I had just finished preparing my breakfast which included a steaming hot cup of tea and placed it on the kitchen table. As I was about to take my seat at the table, I looked across the hallway and saw my grandson in such a unique pose. He stood with both hands outstretched above his head resting on the grandfather's clock in the hallway, quietly admiring the trinkets that were arranged on the base of the inside of the clock. I thought to myself, this is what I can only describe as a "Kodak Moment," I must capture it on film. I left my breakfast on the table and ran to the family room, quickly grabbed my camera from the mantel piece, with the intention of taking his picture. As I turned around intending to return to the hallway to snap the picture, the scene that presented itself to me caused me to freeze on the spot. In the split-second I turned my back; Jacob was through looking at the trinkets and was standing beside the table with his face looking upwards directly under the scalding hot cup of tea, with his hand on the handle of the cup. It was a horrible sight! I knew instantly I could never get to him in time, and that he was about to bring the cup and its very hot contents right into his face. I also knew at that moment I needed the help of the Lord, and I needed it fast. From the very depths of my soul, I cried out as loudly as I could, "JESUS OF NAZARETH." I cannot tell you exactly what happened next, but by the time I unfroze and got to him he was no longer holding the cup's handle, there was a small amount of tea splashed in the saucer and he was crying. I instantly scooped him up in my arms and went to Shelley who was sitting in the family room. Her back was turned to us, so she had no idea what had just taken place. Of course, she heard the commotion and by the time I got to her, her eyes were wide with confusion. She asked what had just happened. I responded that Jacob was about to empty the cup of hot tea on his face. She then said to me "Mom, the moment you called on the Lord, I felt a mighty rushing breeze rush right past me and into the kitchen". I just said to her, "That's my Jesus." The scripture says: "Call on me in the day of trouble and I will deliver thee, and thou shalt glorify me." **Psalms 50:15.**

It was about 6:00 p.m. that evening when my grand-daughter Talia and I attended the New Year's Eve service at my church Liberty Full Gospel Chapel. We had just been dropped off by my husband for the service, with the plan being my daughter Jacinth will join us after work and then we three will drive home together. It was a delightful service in which members gave testimonies of the blessings that the Lord had bestowed on them over the past year (2015). I had just given my testimony and returned to my seat when I knew something was wrong with me, very wrong. I began hearing a noise in my head, as though a freight train was moving around. Another woman had gotten up to give her testimony, but I could not determine what language she was speaking; I could not understand her. I then became very disoriented; I could not tell whether I was sitting in the church for ten minutes or four hours. Total confusion engulfed me. I got up and went to the back of the church and phoned Joe to come to take me home. I just wanted to lie down in my bed. He could not understand why I sounded so confused. He asked what was the matter with me but I was unable to articulate what was happening to me, I just told him I was not feeling well. He then reminded me that Jacinth was on her way to the church to meet us. I hung up the phone from him and then phoned Jacinth telling her the same thing. She too asked what was wrong, and yet I did not know what to say to her, I simply repeated what I had just said to her dad, that I was not feeling well. She told me she was on her way. I got off the phone with her and went to the door to get my car (remember I did not drive a car there) and was astonished that it was dark outside; the darkness frightened me. Somehow in my head I am thinking this should not be; why is it dark outside it should be daylight, I do not drive at night.

Because I was so utterly confused and could not understand what was happening to me, I went back into the church and sat down in my seat. I started feeling worse and worse and the noise in my head continued. Soon the pastor brought the service to a close. I was hoping he would make an altar call for those who needed prayer which was the custom in that church, but he did not. He concluded the service then blessed the meal (we were having a potluck dinner that evening) and invited everyone downstairs to partake. All I could do was rest my head on the chair in front of me and call on the Lord for help. As I lifted my head I saw the pastor's wife Meera, standing in the aisle looking at me. I beckoned to her. When she asked me what was the matter I told her there was utter confusion in my head. She immediately called the pastor over where they laid hands on me and pastor Billy prayed for me. Miraculously, as soon as the pastor concluded the prayer I felt normal again. (The pastor's wife later told me that as she was sitting on the platform, she just knew in the spirit that there was something seriously wrong with me.) All this while Jacinth was phoning dad to ask what was wrong with me; he had no idea. I later learned that as she arrived at the church, Sister Meera was waiting for her at the door with a comforting answer to her question, "What's wrong with my mom?"

"Don't worry, your mom is fine, we prayed for her." All this while I was downstairs enjoying the meal; apparently my brain did not register all the confusion that had just taken place.

When we got home my husband kept staring at me in disbelief, as though he could not understand my nonchalant attitude. Remember, about two hours ago, I had phoned him in a state of confusion, and now I sauntered through the door as though nothing amiss had taken place and all is well. But to be honest, I could not even recall what had happened a few hours ago, nor could I understand why he seemed to be annoyed with me.

The following day Shelley, who was not at church, phoned me to find out what was the matter with me the previous night. I then said to her it was nothing and that her sister should not have bothered to mention it to her at all, because I was fine. She then scolded me. 'Whenever anything is wrong with me you are always there for me, you want to know I am doing well. It works both ways I want to know you are okay and expect you to take care of yourself.'

With that scolding I thought to myself, she is right; it is quite some time since I checked my blood pressure, perhaps there might be a problem there. I then got out my machine and sat beside Joe who was lying in bed. The blood pressure reading shocked us both. Joe immediately sat up in bed and declared, "That's high, that's high". It was 250/150 mmHg, yes, it was dangerously high. I ran to my medicine cabinet and actually took a double dose of my medication. Perhaps that too was not wise on my part, but I wanted those figures reduced ASAP. My BP level was in the stroke region as my sister-in-law Grace who is a nurse later informed me. It was really a miracle of the Lord that I did not suffer a massive stroke.

My advice to anyone who is on blood pressure medication is this: Be vigilant and take your medication as prescribed by your doctor, and do not neglect to check your blood pressure regularly. I am even more vigilant now because I do not want a repeat of that frightening experience. Thank God for the prayers of my pastors and thank God the incident happened at church!

I was driving west on McGillivray Blvd. in the fall of 2019. I was driving on the outer lane of the highway going at approximately sixty kilometers per hour. The road ahead of me appeared to be clear when suddenly after a few yards my car came to a complete stop. That put me in a state of confusion; I never stopped my car, there was no reason for me to stop but there I was stopped in the middle of the road. I was conscious of the fact that my car had stopped in alignment with another vehicle to my left. To my consternation a man suddenly appeared walking nonchalantly in front of my car, who apparently had just walked in front of the car to my left. I thought to myself what a foolish man, how dare he just walk across this busy street with no concern for his safety. By this time, the man had cleared both cars and was on the side of the road. I soon became aware of the fact, that the car to my left began driving off, but I was still stopped in the middle of the highway, confused, I guess. I then heard the Holy Spirit speak to me, "It's your turn to go now." It was a gentle voice, like the tone I would use when I am speaking to my little grand-daughter Kaliyah. I obeyed; I knew it was the Lord. In the scriptures the Lord says, "My sheep know my voice," **John10: 27-28** but I was still unaware of what just happened. After I had driven a few yards, the Lord spoke to me again. "I want you to look back and see what I just delivered you from." As I looked back through the rear-view mirror, to my astonishment, I realized that I was just stopped at a pedestrian crossing which I did not see at all and would have driven right into that pedestrian. The Lord knew that I did not see him, and He stopped my car right on time for me. When I realized what had just taken place, I began praising the Lord aloud all to the way to my home. It took me a couple of days before I felt composed enough to relate the incident to my family. **Psalms 91:15** states "I will be with him in trouble; I will deliver him." He delivered me from trouble, even though I was unaware that I was in trouble. A friend later told me of a near accident that took place at that same pedestrian crossing. The general complaint I heard was that the crossing lights were situated too high, making it difficult for drivers to see them.

Nine

Having your own children to love and take care of is a blessing from the Lord; but having grandchildren as well, is a double blessing from above. As my grand babies came along, I viewed their arrival as one of the second-best gifts that the Lord can give to a mother. I have six of them and it thrills my heart to hear them call me "grandma." I sometimes chuckle to myself at the thought that these little people are a part of me going forward into the future. I try my best to teach them good Christian values whenever I can. Each summer when I have them all together, I usually instruct them in things of the Lord, and have them commit certain verses of scripture to memory; The Lord's prayer; The Shepherd's Psalm; **John 3:16** (A salvation scripture).

One morning as I lay in my bed, I thought to myself that I would teach them the Ten Commandments this summer. At that point, the Spirit of the Lord spoke to me: He instructed me that I should teach them to accept Him as their Personal Lord and Saviour, as opposed to teaching them the Ten Commandments. Later that month when I got them all together, I led them all to the Lord. They all invited Jesus into their hearts except Kaliyah, who was just three years old. Praise God, now they all know that they are blood-washed, saved, and born again, **John 3: 3-8** and that Jesus loves them.

As mothers and grandmothers, we need to pray for our households. We need to lift them up before the Lord daily, and to entrust them into His care. He is a God who loves us, who listens to our petitions and answers our prayers.

You might notice that I speak quite a bit about the Holy Spirit guiding me in situations. What I would like to share with you is that once an individual is saved and has become a believer, and has received the precious gift of salvation, he/she is sealed with the Holy Spirit of promise. **Ephesians 1:13** He becomes our spiritual partner, our moral compass and guide. He leads us into all truth. On a daily basis He keeps us and hides us from danger. We all need to thank God the Father for sending Him to us from above. **John 14:26.**

When I first decided to write my memoirs, I had no intention of sharing my testimonies with anyone, nor relating any of my experiences with the Lord, because I believed they were personal between myself and Him. As I progressed with my book however, I soon realized that it was impossible to extricate my daily life from my spiritual life, because they are both entwined. At times, I even wonder whether the Lord gave me those experiences in Him, so that I could chronicle them, that others can read and be blessed as well; knowing what He has done for me He is willing to do for them also.

We have an awesome God. Once we have surrendered to Him we can talk to Him and experience Him every day. We can lean on Him, depend on Him, and He would always come through for us. As we exercise our faith in Him daily, He will bring peace and comfort into our lives.

After having made the above statements; I hasten to inform the reader that the life of a Christian is not always one that is pain-free, worry-free, and problem-free; nothing is further from the truth. The scripture states in **Psalms 34:19** "Many are the afflictions of the righteous." As Christians we all experience situations; sometimes we are on the mountain tops of life and at other times we are in the valleys, but as the scripture continues, "but the Lord delivers us out of them all." We just need to believe His word and trust Him.

In my book I chose not to include my valley experiences, because they would not bless you in anyway. My intention is that this book should inspire you, bless your heart, and increase your faith in Him. At present my faith is still out there in the field: I am trusting Him to heal me of high blood pressure one day. Until then I will follow the instructions of my doctor, (Christianity is practical) and still trust in God to heal me in His time. He is our healer.

My hope is that everyone who reads this book will be encouraged in the Lord. I strongly believe that He wants me to emphasize the salvation experience, because salvation takes us into eternity with Him: It is a free gift, and it is available for everyone today. The scripture states that whosoever will, may come. Each and every one of us needs to have that experience: Surrendering to Jesus and inviting Him into our hearts. Many terms are used in the scriptures to express the salvation concept: It is sometimes referred to as being "born again," or "the new birth," or being "saved." In essence, they all refer to the life-changing experience that follows an encounter with the Saviour. It is of the utmost importance to note at this time, that I am not an advocate for any particular Church or Christian religion; I am speaking of an individual having a personal relationship with the living God.

We may not know what the future holds. There is so much uncertainty in this world; but we do know who holds the future - that's God. He secured my future and your future by sending His Son Jesus Christ to this earth from heaven, to take my sins and yours to the cross of Calvary. He died, shed His blood, was buried then God raised Him to life. He is alive today and He is willing to forgive you of your sins if you will just ask Him. **John 3:16** states, "God so loved the world that He gave his only begotten Son, that whosoever believes in Him should not perish but have everlasting life."

If you have never trusted Jesus as your saviour, you can do that right now and be sure that your future is secure in His hands.

JUST PRAY THIS PRAYER: *"Dear God, I'm a sinner. I am sorry for my sins. Forgive me. I believe that Jesus Christ is your Son, and I now trust Him as my Lord and Saviour. I am willing to follow Him from this day forward. Thank you, Lord, for saving me."*

If you just prayed this prayer, and you believe in your heart that God is real and has heard your prayer, then you are saved. **Romans 10:9** "If thou shalt confess with thy mouth the Lord Jesus, and shalt believe in thine heart that God hath raised him from the dead, thou shalt be saved." Just trust Him and He will begin to direct your life from this moment forward. All that He accomplished on the cross of Calvary some two thousand years ago for all mankind, will now become a reality in your life.

All Humanity needs to know that because of Adam's transgression, sin has passed unto each and every one who is born in this world. The scripture states, Romans 3:23 "All have sinned and fallen short of the glory of God." We ALL need a Saviour to set us free from the power of sin. No one should ever depart this world, without having their sins washed away by the precious blood of Jesus.

I thank God for the day of my salvation and the assurance of eternal life with Him. I wish that same experience for everyone who reads this book.

Be Blessed!

EPILOGUE

Salvation Scriptures:

Acts 4:12 – *Neither is there salvation in any other: for there is none other name under heaven given among men, whereby we must be saved.*

Acts 16:31 – *Believe on the Lord Jesus Christ, and thou shalt be saved, and thy house.*

John 3:16 – *For God so loved the world, that He gave His only begotten son, that whosoever believeth in Him should not perish, but have everlasting life.*

John 10:9 – *I am the door: by me if any man enters in, he shall be saved, and shall go in and out, and find pasture.*

John 11:25 & 26: – *I am the resurrection, and the life: he that believeth in me, though he were dead, yet shall he live: And whosoever liveth and believeth in me shall never die.*

John 14:6 – *I am the way, the truth, and the life: no man cometh unto the father but by me.*

John 3:3 – *Verily, verily, I say unto thee, except a man be born again, he cannot see the kingdom of God.*

Romans 5:8 – *But God commendeth his love toward us, in that, while we were yet sinners, Christ died for us.*

Romans 6:23 – *For the wages of sin is death; but the gift of God is eternal life through Jesus Christ our Lord.*

Romans 10:9 & 10 – *If thou shalt confess with thy mouth the Lord Jesus, and shalt believe in thine heart that God raised him from the dead, thou shalt be saved. For with the heart man believeth unto righteousness; and with the mouth confession is made unto salvation.*

ACKNOWLEDGMENTS

Writing and self-publishing a book has been uncharted territory for me. My desire to leave behind a legacy of spiritual significance through sharing my story, has been the motivation which kept me forging ahead, along this unfamiliar and sometimes difficult road.

I wish to thank my husband Joe who dutifully and willingly accepted the task of driving me from "pillar to post" as I tried to navigate my way through this unfamiliar territory, to bring this project to fruition.

Special thanks to pastor James Barber of Faith Bible Church for taking the time out of his very busy schedule to read my manuscript. Thanks so much for your kind words of encouragement.

My friend and neighbour Debbie Stewart provided me with a mountain of support even though she might not be aware of it. The interest she showed in my manuscript was heart-warming: I sent it to her via e-mail one evening in the summer of 2022, she lay in bed that night and read the entire manuscript, over 17,200 words, overnight. She then e-mailed me her comments the following morning and at the same time invited me over to her home for coffee where she wanted "to go over a few edits" with me. She then donned her teacher's hat (she is a teacher by profession) where we visited the areas of concern.

I truly welcomed her suggestions: e.g. "You already wrote in a previous chapter that you suffered from asthma. There is no need to repeat it here again, remove it." To which I duly responded, "Yes ma'am." Thanks so much Debbie.

Brother Phillip Charles's comments and suggestions during and after reading the manuscript were both helpful and uplifting. His suggestion of keeping the timelines in an orderly fashion was well received. His words of encouragement as I met with him, and his wife Wanda on Sunday mornings after church, truly blessed my heart. Thanks so much to you both.

Thanks to my brother-in-law Hamid. It was quite a joy talking with him after he read the manuscript. His uplifting words still resound with me. Of particular amusement to him was the incident in high school, (over some sixty years ago) when his wife Vestine and I created a colossal hullabaloo in the school, which frightened the European Nun out of her wits!

Special thanks to my daughter Jacinth who provided both moral and technical support which I so desperately needed from time to time, particularly in this new age of technology. From the first day I decided to write my memoir, hers has been a loud voice of encouragement in this endeavour which I really appreciate. My granddaughter Talia did an excellent job of proof-reading the entire manuscript. She has been my harshest critic. She read through it with an eagle eye and was able to pinpoint every last error or inconsistency which I had missed, even though I read it through several times. She did her grandma proud! She is also responsible for the cover design of this book.

To my forever friend Victoria Forde, my sincere thanks and gratitude for the support you gave to me. Before I dared to show my manuscript to anyone else, I had Victoria read it. I just wanted the assurance that what I was writing was worth the while. Her strong vote of confidence was all I needed to keep me forging ahead. I call her my forever friend because she has always been that. As far back as I can recall she was always there; playing dolly house with me and my two little sisters as kids, and sometimes spending the weekend at our home. Our parents were friends. My sisters have all passed on to glory now, but she stands in the gap for me as a sister and I for her.

Special thanks to Mike Taniguchi of Hignell Book Printing for his patience as we worked together to get this book printed. His skill, his knowledge, support and guidance were instrumental in moving this project along. It was indeed a pleasure working with him.

Last but not least, I would like to express my appreciation to you the reader who took the time to read my life story. I trust God that it will be a blessing in your life.

www.ingramcontent.com/pod-product-compliance
Lightning Source LLC
Chambersburg PA
CBHW041147110526
44590CB00027B/4156